The Patio Portfolio
An Inspirational Design Guide

David R. Smith
Interlocking Concrete Pavement Institute

Schiffer Publishing Ltd

4880 Lower Valley Road, Atglen, PA 19310 USA

ICPI
INTERLOCKING CONCRETE
PAVEMENT INSTITUTE

Library of Congress Cataloging-in-Publication Data

Smith, David R. (David Randolph), 1953-
The patio portfolio : an inspirational design guide / by David R. Smith.
p. cm.
ISBN 0-7643-2050-5 (pbk.)
1. Patios. I. Title.
TH4970.S5526 2004
728'.93--dc22
2004002557

Cover image courtesy of Cambridge Pavers Inc.
BL: Cambridge Pavers Inc.
BM: Barkman Concrete Ltd.
BR: Superlite Block
Back cover image courtesy of Paver Systems

Designed by Bonnie M. Hensley
Cover design by Bruce Waters
Type set in English111 Presto BT/Zurich Cn BT

ISBN: 0-7643-2050-5
Printed in China

Published by Schiffer Publishing Ltd.
4880 Lower Valley Road
Atglen, PA 19310
Phone: (610) 593-1777; Fax: (610) 593-2002
E-mail: Info@schifferbooks.com

For the largest selection of fine reference books on this and related subjects,
please visit our web site at www.schifferbooks.com
We are always looking for people to write books on new and related subjects. If
you have an idea for a book please contact us at the above address.

This book may be purchased from the publisher.
Include $3.95 for shipping.
Please try your bookstore first.
You may write for a free catalog.

In Europe, Schiffer books are distributed by
Bushwood Books
6 Marksbury Ave.
Kew Gardens
Surrey TW9 4JF England
Phone: 44 (0) 20 8392-8585; Fax: 44 (0) 20 8392-9876
E-mail: info@bushwoodbooks.co.uk
Free postage in the U.K., Europe; air mail at cost.

contents

introduction

Rarely on a pleasant day is it heard, "I think I'll stay indoors today." Besides meeting a basic human need, being outside refreshes and renews. At home, this need is met through patios. The word patio finds its root in ancient Spanish that means untilled land. This suggests a place of rest and relaxation, a place of recovery, even celebration, of being and not sowing or reaping. The Spanish word for patio also means courtyard, a place that is surrounded and protected by the home. It is an outdoor living room embraced and protected by the walls of the house. Images of Mediterranean style homes come to mind—a courtyard filled with a gurgling fountain, a small garden and palm trees enclosed by stucco walls, windows, doors, stairs, clay roof tiles, and stone paving.

Creating your patio as a place to recover and recharge by enjoying the outdoors takes some planning. It starts with answering some questions. What's going to happen in this space? Besides a quiet place to be by yourself, who else will use it? Your spouse? The kids? The neighbors? How will you entertain others and how many can comfortably stand or sit on the patio? Many patios function as a living room with tables and chairs, gardens, fireplaces, and firepits. They can serve as a kitchen with a barbeque grill and a bar, or as a den with a swimming pool, hot tub, pond, fountain, or waterfalls. Chapter 1 entitled The Perfect Patio for You assists in visualizing how your patio might be used and the size and scale required.

It's another room, but outside the house instead of in it. Rooms have entrances, views, floors, walls, and ceilings. Patios have entrances, openings to vistas, and can be enclosed by vegetation or walls. Concrete pavers serve as floors, with segmental concrete, shrubs, and trees as walls. Lofty tree canopies provide ceilings whose leaves resonate with the breeze, as well as arbors, trellises, awnings, and umbrellas.

This book is brought to you by the members of the Interlocking Concrete Pavement Institute (ICPI), who make the floors for patios called concrete pavers. The units are made from crushed stone, sand, and cement. Pigment is added and various finishes are applied to give them specific stone-like characteristics. Because each manufacturer uses different local materials and production processes, paver appearance varies with each manufacturer. Therefore, paving products take on a character specific to the region where it's manufactured.

The members of the ICPI would be pleased to provide information on the shapes, patterns, colors, and finishes available in your area. Many companies can provide product catalogs and they have projects displayed on their web sites. Many distribute through home center stores, landscape, or masonry supply stores. Viewing paver samples will give you a better idea of the color and texture options. A look through Chapter 2 on Applying Patterns, Textures, and Colors will help refine your choices before visiting with a contractor or paver supplier.

Environmental design considerations are essential to the planning process. These might include buffering noise, shading and welcoming the sun, blocking wind, dealing with drainage, and connection to other places in the backyard. Such places can be driveways, garages and other buildings, playgrounds, paths, grassed areas, woods, streams, lakes, rivers, or beaches. As you carefully review the pictures in the book your sensitivity to these design influences will arise. Your preferences will become clearer as you consider each of these in the context of your backyard. Chapter 3, called From the Patio to the Backyard, will assist in considering how to relate the patio to other things in the yard.

A great way to start is to layout the shape of the patio with a garden hose. If that's not long enough, string will work. Anchor it so the wind doesn't move it. One of the first rules of laying out a patio is that the space required for everything will be bigger than you first imagine. Leave plenty of room around tables and chairs, barbeques, fireplaces, hot tubs, ponds, and swimming pools. Speaking of pools, they offer opportunities for some of the most creative designs. Chapter 4 on Patios with Pools provides a wealth of ideas. Chapter 5 shows treatments of patios as outdoor environments. They become personal places of escape to recharge with help from fountains, fireplaces, barbeque facilities, and ponds.

Many experienced concrete paver installation contractors and some landscaping companies can provide design guidance and offer suggestions on the shape of the patio layout. All can offer a range of concrete paver shapes, colors, and textures—many of which are shown in this book. Be sure to obtain prices from at least two contractors, and be sure each has a portfolio of projects to show you. It will provide ideas specific to the potentials and limitations of your backyard. A warranty should be offered for the materials and labor.

The contractor should be an ICPI certified concrete paver installer. This means they have taken a class on the industry standards for constructing residential projects and have passed an exam. While certification recognizes a contractor's understanding of industry standards, it does not guarantee good work. Your assurance for a quality job is from contractor-supplied references and visiting the contractor's recent projects. Certification means the contractor is serious enough about his or her work that time was taken to study and take a test on industry standards. It is one assurance among these that you will receive a quality project. The ICPI web site offers a great brochure called the Consumer Guide to assist you in evaluating contractors and their proposals. It can be downloaded from the Homeowner section at www.icpi.org.

All patios should have a minimum four-inch (200 mm) thick, compacted, crushed stone base, a layer of bedding sand, and edge restraints firmly holding the pavers in place. The base may be thicker in colder climates. The minimum thickness of the concrete pavers should be 2 3/8-inches (60 mm). The bedding sand should be an inch (25 mm) thick. Limestone screenings and stone dust are not recommended. Edge restraints are typically plastic fastened to the compacted base or are made with concrete. Of course, the wall of the house can serve as a restraint.

In some situations, concrete pavers can be placed on a thin layer of bedding sand directly over an existing concrete patio slab. Slightly thicker pavers are glued to the concrete slab and function as edge restraints. In adding the sand and pavers, sufficient vertical clearance should be available between the top of the pavers and the bottom of the doors. No matter what base is under the patio, the surface should drain away from the house.

If you're interested in installing your own pavers, keep the project small, say under 300 square feet or 30 square meters. Patios up to this size can usually get built in a few weekends. Anything larger than that will require specialized equipment that professional contractors will have to complete the project quickly. Step-by step guidelines for installing your own patio can be obtained from ICPI members and from the Homeowner section of the ICPI web site, www.icpi.org. In addition, you can review some patio project ideas from across North America while you're perusing the site.

Like adding another room to your house, patios add to its value now and when the house is sold. We hope the projects in this book help you get the most value for your time, efforts, and money now, while increasing future resale value. We hope that results create a place to rest, renew, and recharge so that that the times when, and places where you till the land will yield much produce.

David R. Smith
Interlocking Concrete Pavement Institute
Washington, DC

the perfect patio for you

Because the patio is an extension of the home, its design is as important as any room inside. Before you start planning, you should first think about how you will use your patio. Will your patio serve mainly as a stage for the pool, with some lounge chairs and a small barbecuing area? Perhaps you entertain frequently, in which case you'll need lots of space for tables and chairs, or even an outdoor bar. Maybe you want a small, quiet nook where you can relax in the fresh air. Whatever purposes your patio will serve, they should determine its final design. This chapter will help you visualize what your perfect patio will look like and will also help you think about how you will use it.

A wooded vista is best enjoyed from this bean shaped landing *Courtesy of Interlock Concrete Products, Inc.*

Beautifully crafted ironwork supports a yellow awning, casting patterned shadows on the patio floor, and creating an outdoor room reminiscent of an Italian piazza. *Courtesy of Bolduc*

Circular patterns extend outward like ripples on water where patio meets path and porch. A small tree in the island of mulch will one day provide shade to those who sit below. *Courtesy of Bolduc*

A combination of rounded and squared edges give a unique look to a multi-toned patio. The patio's small size still provides room for multiple seating areas. *Courtesy of Interlock Concrete Products, Inc.*

An raised circle of pavers provides a perfect little spot for an outdoor dining area. *Courtesy of Interlock Concrete Products, Inc.*

A walkway snakes through a landscaped yard, climaxing with a circular patio right in front of the house. *Courtesy of Interlock Concrete Products, Inc.*

A little round patio behind the house is an escape from the stresses of everyday life. *Courtesy of Interlock Concrete Products, Inc.*

Young trees that line the edge of patio closest to the neighbors' house will provide lots of privacy as they grow tall in the coming years. *Courtesy of EP Henry*

A walkway ends in a dramatic circular pattern, drawing attention to the entryway of this home. Landscaping in blues, greens, and yellows complements the rustic gray pavers. *Courtesy of Mutual Materials*

A small patio is made especially cozy by the addition of an ivy-covered arbor and gurgling koi pond. *Courtesy of EP Henry*

Paver patterns can add excitement to the straight lines of brick walls and plank fences, which give this patio a feeling of intimacy. *Courtesy of Angelus Block Co., Inc.*

A zigzagging patio gives the impression of space in this enclosed area. *Courtesy of Peterson Bros.*

This small patio sits right up against the house, convenient for the owners who host many dinner parties during the summer. The proximity of the house to the patio allows easy access to the kitchen. Two tones give a checkerboard feel to the patio. *Courtesy of Oaks Concrete Products*

The owners of this house wanted a place to drink a glass of coffee and read the paper in the early morning sunshine. *Courtesy of Techo Bloc*
←

An attractive pattern adds appeal to a small and simple patio. *Courtesy of EP Henry*
→

A wide, raised patio offers endless options for outdoor living. A table, some chairs, and a gas grill would make this a great entertaining space. *Courtesy of Oaks Concrete Products*

Two large circles of pavers provide lots of useable space, and are visually pleasing from any view. *Courtesy of Interlock Concrete Products, Inc.*

An integrated patio/walkway project complements the arches in the home's architecture. *Courtesy of Cambridge Pavers Inc.*

Random white pavers punctuate a herringbone pattern on this expanse of patio. With the addition of a table and chairs, this patio will be the ultimate summer dining spot. *Courtesy of EP Henry*

Residents can pull up a chair and enjoy the radiating warmth produced from the fire pit built into their expansive backyard patio. *Courtesy of Mutual Materials*

Half walls define an intimate gathering space close to the house while providing seating. Beyond, an additional skirt of matching pavers provides space into which a party can spill. *Courtesy of EP Henry*

Planters are placed among the pavers in this shady promenade. The contractor was able to build around the existing trees to provide the cool retreat. *Courtesy of Paver Systems*

Privacy is retained in this backyard leisure spot, with large boulders lining the perimeter of the patio and trees at the edge of the yard. *Courtesy of Oldcastle Architectural*

Rectangles and squares of stone combine to form a delightfully round outdoor living space. *Courtesy of Kirchner Block and Brick*

Steps smooth the descent to a pool in this backyard Eden. *Courtesy of Techo Bloc*

The homeowners wanted a patio big enough for a pool and entertaining friends. Redwood-stained furniture brings out the red pavers. Beyond, flowered landscaping softens the transition from patio to lawn. *Courtesy of Cambridge Pavers Inc.*
←

Half-circle stairs descend to a patio area, and a ripple seems to spread to the rounded edge. A patio that skirts the house seems to be separated into two areas by the house's corner. *Courtesy of Techo Bloc*
→

Multiple levels of patio create separate areas for different uses. A stone surround means less maintenance and more time spent soaking in the spa. *Courtesy of Cambridge Pavers Inc.*
→

Patio furniture decorates as well as provides a place to drink morning coffee or an evening glass of merlot. *Courtesy of Bolduc*
←

Opposite page:
Long, smooth pavers indicate transitions between different areas of the patio. *Courtesy of Peterson Bros.*

Despite the fact that this home's first floor was above ground level, the contractor was able to give the owners easy access to their backyard patio. By constructing a small landing, they were able to avoid large costs without sacrificing aesthetics. *Courtesy of Unilock*

A patio curves around the adjacent house. It's the perfect location for a hearty summer night of good company and grilling. *Courtesy of R.I. Lampus*

Comfy chairs offer an irresistible temptation in a backyard elegantly hard-scaped in curving patterns of honeyed concrete stone. *Courtesy of EP Henry*

A process of tumbling prematurely aged these concrete pavers, adding texture and the comfort of well-worn jeans to the appearance of a new patio area. *Courtesy of PaverModule*

A pillar of coordinating stones holds the roof up over a cobblestone-like patio. *Courtesy of Orco Block Company, Inc.*

Three colors make up the ground-work for this covered dining area. *Courtesy of Paver Systems* →

Pavers create a concrete foundation for a porch. The comfort of a rocking chair vies with crochet mallets for the residents' attention. *Courtesy of PaverModule* ←

Concrete pavers provide this home a welcoming
entrance, in addition to cozy nook to sit and chat
with a friend. *Courtesy of PaverModule*

A circular pattern amidst this front
patio serves as an initial welcome
mat before you reach the door.
Courtesy of Pavestone Company

A patio in the front yard makes for a grand and welcoming entrance. *Courtesy of EP Henry*

Smooth textured patterns provide a great outdoor play space and a welcome committee. *Courtesy of Oaks Concrete Products.*

Opposite page, top:
A concrete paver driveway extends all the way to the front door, making room for an outdoor lounge. A rectangle of brick-colored pavers accentuates an otherwise ordinary patio, drawing attention to the space. *Courtesy of Kirchner Block and Brick*

Bottom: A simple ironwork fence along the inner patio's edge lends a traditional feel to an otherwise modern setting. Such an expansive patio in the front yard means less time spent landscaping. *Courtesy of Bolduc*

A raised patio substitutes for a deck, wrapping around this house. *Courtesy of Site Technologies* →

A cozy little patio was carved out to capitalize on a lakefront view. The retaining walls that hold back the hills also offer seating should the party of two receive company. *Courtesy of Borgert Products, Inc.* ←

CHAPTER TWO
choosing and applying patterns, textures, & colors

Now that you've thought about how you will use your patio, it's time to think about what you want your patio to look like. Pavers come in a wide range of colors, styles, and textures that can be mixed and matched to create a style that complements your home and your personality. From classic elegance to contemporary flair, any look can be achieved depending on the pavers you choose. This chapter offers a visual smorgasbord of paver patterns, textures, and colors to help you start thinking about what your patio should look like.

All photos on this page are Courtesy of ICPI

Courtesy of RMC

Courtesy of ICPI

Courtesy of ICPI

Courtesy of Pavestone Company

Courtesy of Pavestone Company

Courtesy of Pavestone Company

Courtesy of Pavestone Company

Interspersed black paving stones within a field of brick-red octagons creates a checkerboard effect. *Courtesy of RMC*

The pastel-toned pavers give a soft look to this patio, adding to the cozy feel provided by a stone wall. *Courtesy of Abbotsford Concrete Products, Ltd.*

Interlocking hammerhead pavers create an artful surround to this courtyard setting, centered around a small, stone-lined fish pond. *Courtesy of RMC*

Columns with a faux finish give the impression of age, while supporting a roof that provides relief from the scorching Arizona sun. A mix of materials used in this patio project adds dimension and interest to the finished product. *Courtesy of Belgard-Permacon*

A multi-tiered patio with an exciting paver pattern adds depth and style to the back of the home, and provides a better view of the distant lake. *Courtesy of Kirchner Block and Brick*
←

Matching concrete capstone and pavers grace a walk and patio, creating the illusion that the entire setting was cut from natural stone. *Courtesy of Techo Bloc*
→

Transitions between patterns add visual interest. Here, larger flagstones indicate the beginning of the covered patio area. An ornately decorated concrete bench provides seating for these homeowners to enjoy their backyard foliage and sculpture. *Courtesy of Flagstone Pavers*

Natural-toned pavers and strong columns set the stage for a tranquil outdoor retreat. *Courtesy of Flagstone Pavers*

Long and slender pavers were used to create the pattern on the landings that lead to the patio. These imply movement, while the larger pavers that form a simpler pattern on the patio lend a feeling of stillness and tranquility. *Courtesy of EP Henry*

A white picket fence, some topiary, and a bit of seasonal landscaping add flavor and character to a backyard patio. *Courtesy of Orco Block Company, Inc.*

This patio pattern is electric, yet not too busy for a big patio like this one. *Courtesy of EP Henry*

A fountain becomes the focal point of a colorfully laid patio, complete with color coordinating flowers! *Courtesy of Oaks Concrete Products*

Big and little squares harmonize to form a stylish courtyard. *Courtesy of Pavestone Company*

Top: *Courtesy of Flagstone Pavers*
Bottom: Cut into a contrasting ground of darker gray, a circle of pavers creates a center of interest. *Courtesy of PaverModule*

Overlapping circles welcome guests to this outdoor
dining area. *Courtesy of Flagstone Pavers*

A circle of pavers designates a seating area. *Courtesy of Interlock Paving Systems, Inc.*

The design within this patio was meant to mimic a wheel; the spokes all meeting in the center to draw attention to the attractive outdoor space. *Courtesy of Paveloc Industries, Inc.*

A circle of pavers demarcates the center this fabulous entryway. *Courtesy of PaverModule*

Right and opposite page:
Concentric squares define the central gathering points for a spread of patio. *Courtesy of PaverModule*

Gray dissects pink, with three patterns varying the mix in this formal surround for a patio fountain. *Courtesy of PaverModule*

This patio is enjoyed under the sun, moon, or stars, as depicted by a unique poolside celestial design. *Courtesy of R.I. Lampus*

Large and small rectangles combine poolside for a delightful visual effect, while bullnose coping creates a softer effect for these poolside stairs. *Courtesy of ICPI*

An interlocking assembly of pavers creates a parquet pattern, fancy flooring for an outdoor play area. *Courtesy of PaverModule*
←

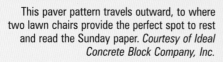

This paver pattern travels outward, to where two lawn chairs provide the perfect spot to rest and read the Sunday paper. *Courtesy of Ideal Concrete Block Company, Inc.*
→

Hexagons and six-point stars in white and terra cotta create a
unique and interesting pathway to this home. Rectangular bricks
make for attractive edging. *Courtesy of Oaks Concrete Products*

Waves of reds and white mimic the ocean waves not far beyond this
tropical refuge. *Courtesy of Paver Systems*

Multi-colored pavers create eye-pleasing patterns. *Courtesy of Paver Systems*

A large courtyard is enhanced by concrete paving and pillars, along with enormous planters and lighting. *Courtesy of PaverModule*

Tumbled pavers provide an aged and refined look. *Courtesy of Flagstone Pavers*

A rough finish creates the rustic feeling sought by these homeowners. *Courtesy of Techo Bloc*

A medley of gray and rust tones adds interest to an expanse of paved area. *Courtesy of PaverModule*

Rough edges give concrete pavers the appearance of natural stone.
Courtesy of Techo Bloc

Whether serving as a driveway, walkway, or patio, pavers add an interesting touch to any landscape. *Courtesy of PaverModule*

A half-moon patterned patio continues beyond the steps before branching off to different parts of the yard. *Courtesy of R.I. Lampus*

Larger, square paver stones were used to break up an expanse of patio and to help define zones. *Courtesy of PaverModule*

Tumbled pavers are sandwiched between stripes of red brick pavers, for a contrasting sense of old and new. *Courtesy of PaverModule*

Cobblestone effect is created using tumbled pavers. *Courtesy of PaverModule*

Three sizes of rectangular pavers are randomly set in the long lines of this sprawling patio area, adding texture and interest. *Courtesy of Barkman Concrete*

CHAPTER THREE
from the patio to the backyard

Once you begin considering design options for the construction of your patio, it is important that you think holistically about the patio, the home, and the backyard. Because the patio is a transitional space that links the home with the outdoors, you should think about how it fits into the larger picture. Do you want a patio that sits right next to the home? Perhaps you want a path that runs from the backdoor to a more isolated patio that is more a part of the outdoors than a part of the home. Will your patio spill right out into the yard, will it have walls or stairs? As you flip through this chapter, you'll get a sense of the different ways in which the patio forms part of a larger outdoor environment.

Sturdy pillars topped with elegant ironwork and lanterns add grace this patio which spills out into the backyard with some steps and a landing. *Courtesy of R.I. Lampus*

A retaining wall lined with colorful flowering bushes defines the edge of this patio. Various patterns in a patio can set the tone for how it will be used. A circle implies a place to sit and stay, while the rows imply movement. *Courtesy of EP Henry*

The spa was separated from the main patio area by a knee-high wall. The large pots of plants that flank the stairs that connect the two patio areas provide a heightened sense of privacy. *Courtesy of EP Henry*

A circular patio by the sea seems the perfect setting for a Druid's ceremony. A pillared wall separates this patio from its ocean backdrop. *Courtesy of Abbotsford Concrete Products, Ltd.*

A half wall around the patio creates a sense of intimacy, and also provides built-in seating.
Courtesy of Unilock

A Spanish-style stucco wall separates a patio from the outside world. Rectangular pavers in a straight line help to make an expansive patio feel smaller. This effect is also achieved through the use of planters in the center and a gray border along its edge. *Courtesy of Basalite*
←

Plants along the edge of an elevated patio decorate and warn guests that the end is near…*Courtesy of EP Henry*
→

Layers of patio unfold into a grassy lawn from the slightly elevated backdoor. *Courtesy of EP Henry*

A double line of differing size pavers line the outer edge of a patio, presenting a clear signal that there is a drop off. *Courtesy of RMC*

A half wall snugs a circular patio. It doesn't take a great stretch of the imagination to turn this handy tea table into a prop for a princess's castle. *Courtesy of EP Henry*

Stairs lead up to the top of the land-scaped hill and add a feeling of space to this patio. *Courtesy of EP Henry*

A semi-circular half wall defines an *au natural* breakfast nook. *Courtesy of EP Henry*

Boulders set the boundaries for fence and poolside patio of this secluded backyard paradise. *Courtesy of Techo Bloc*

Half-circles provide a landing and steps from home to patio, flanked by matching circular planters. The patio flows away in a free-form shape, a natural spill of hardscaping area into the swath of green beyond. *Courtesy of Barkman Concrete*

Rather than fill the entire space with pavers, these homeowners decided to create a unique and attractive design throughout their lawn, rather than over top of it. *Courtesy of Mutual Materials*

The patio is a great place to sit and enjoy the colorfully changing seasons. A raised wall serves as a planter and divider between patio and lawn. *Courtesy of Kirchner Block and Brick*

Away from all the action, this quiet bench and table are the perfect companions for those who seek solitude. A landscaped border around the patio eases the transition to the yard. *Courtesy of Genest Concrete*

Flowers sandwiched between a raised patio and matching path add appeal. *Courtesy of Ideal Concrete Block Company, Inc.*

Pavers in a darker tone were used to create borders and geometric patterns. The decorative attention adds elegance to this patio. *Courtesy of EP Henry*

The kids can energetically play in the lawn while the adults watch and relax from this patio's benches. A path leads the way from the house. *Courtesy of EP Henry*

Potted plants line the path to a patio tucked away behind a landscaped retaining wall, adding dimension to this backyard hideaway. *Courtesy of Bolduc*

A patio morphs into a pathway that takes travelers to a solitary retreat among the trees. *Courtesy of Belgard-Permacon*

A walkway cuts a clean path through manicured lawn and garden. *Courtesy of Techo Bloc*

Semicircular steps emerge gracefully from multiple levels of retaining walls. Rather than ending abruptly, the patio continues up a landscaped hill as a meandering path. *Courtesy of EP Henry*

Opposite page:
A half-moon patterned patio continues beyond the steps before branching off to different parts of the yard. *Courtesy of R.I. Lampus*

Circular landings categorize this path, which travels up a landscaped hillside to the regal cupola that crowns it. *Courtesy of EP Henry*
→

Lights lend a welcoming feel while adding beauty to the front or back of a house. Circular landings spill onto one another as they descend away from the house. *Courtesy of Kerr Lighting*
←

A patio wraps its way around the basketball court, providing a sense of continuity. *Courtesy of Genest Concrete*

A sweet little entryway patio extends the owner's hospitality to the outdoors. *Courtesy of Unilock*
←

A circular inset acts as a rest stop on a lazy stroll to an enclosed gazebo. The repeating circular patterns are outlined in a matching garden border. *Courtesy of Barkman Concrete*
→

Opposite page:
A gentle walkway from home to back gate
includes space to pause and contemplate.
Courtesy of EP Henry

Loose paths like this one lend themselves to the dreamers
and wanderers. *Courtesy of EP Henry*

A path and landscaped edge give a sense of grandeur and provide
a patio with a real presence in the backyard. *Courtesy of Oaks
Concrete Products*

Paths with a tight construction give a feeling of solidity and
sturdiness, and of having a definite place to go. *Courtesy of
EP Henry*

CHAPTER FOUR
patios for pools

If you're planning on constructing a pool or giving a facelift to your current pool-skirting patio, this chapter will help you start thinking about your design options. Some patios play supporting roles to pools, and others share center stage with them. Large and small, plain and intricately patterned, fenced-in and open to the yard—here you'll find inspiration for your poolside paradise.

A double row of border pavers forms a stylish edge to this expanse of herringbone-pattern patio. *Courtesy of PaverModule*

A border of lights around the pool is a safety feature as well as a decorative one. *Courtesy of Kerr Lighting*

Pavers of different sizes were lined up around this pool, creating the texture and patina of age. *Courtesy of Cambridge Pavers Inc.*

Elongated concrete pavers were designed to be laid three in a row and alternated for a wonderful basket-weave effect. Likewise, the same slender pavers make for elegant edging. These owners wanted plenty pf patio space for future parties. *Courtesy of PaverModule*

Pavers follow the freeform of the pool's shape, lending a feeling of harmony and balance to this skirting patio. *Courtesy of Belgard-Permacon*

The pool takes center stage in this patio, where plants and a few pieces of furniture play supporting roles. *Courtesy of Belgard-Permacon*

A random mix of paver sizes makes for a fascinating patio texture. *Courtesy of Stonetown*

An expanse
of recreation
area
surrounds a
pool in a
waterfront
community.
*Courtesy of
Cambridge
Pavers Inc.*

Rippling around
a free-form pool,
the patio
provides access
to all sides of
the swimming
area, and a dry
place to
congregate.
*Courtesy of
Cambridge
Pavers Inc.*

A herringbone pattern in the paver surround adds emphasis to the curves of a kidney-shaped pool. *Courtesy of Cambridge Pavers Inc.*

Built in a series of squares, pool and patio reflect a harmonious, orderly design. *Courtesy of Cambridge Pavers Inc.*

Locating the seating area at the far side of the pool is a great way to draw people out and to utilize the entire backyard. *Courtesy of Cambridge Pavers Inc.*

A retaining wall elevates the patio, keeping it level with the pool and providing seating for two parties. The drop-off is clearly demarcated with border pavers and tiki torches for safety. *Courtesy of EP Henry*

Elegant columns surround a white marble-like porch, and a patio adds complementary flavor to the color scheme of the architecture. *Courtesy of Paver Systems*

Three colors mix it up in a swirling poolside patio. *Courtesy of Uni-Group*

Slip your feet into the inviting pool, or sun yourself on the
herringbone-patterned patio while gazing off at the distant ocean.
Courtesy of Orco Block Company, Inc

Large and small mingle to create an interesting poolside pattern. *Courtesy of Oaks Concrete Products*

Square pavers contrast with the curving edge of a narrow pool skirt, the contrast emphasized in color. *Courtesy of PaverModule*

A jagged pool edge is emphasized in pavers of various sizes and directional orientation. *Courtesy of PaverModule*

A pool is bordered by multiple paver patterns to add interest and style.
Courtesy of Flagstone Pavers

Opposite page:
A grainy blend of colors make these concrete
squares appear more like exotic cut stone.
Courtesy of PaverModule

©The Greg Wilson Group

A red brick border around the edge of the pool complements the tones of colored pavers. *Courtesy of Flagstone Pavers*

Opposite page:
Wave-shaped pavers are a perfect accompaniment to a free-form pool and spa. *Courtesy of Cambridge Pavers Inc.*

The colorful pavers within this patio follow the contours of the pool, allowing the pool to be the center of attention. *Courtesy of Paver Systems*

Textures and colors complement each other in the hardscaping around a pool. *Courtesy of Barkman Concrete*

CHAPTER FIVE
luxurious patio accessories & amenities

hese days, patios are much more than just places to set a table and some chairs. This chapter will give you some design ideas about how to turn your patio into a fabulous outdoor environment, your own personal retreat that rivals the best resorts. These ponds, fountains, firepits, fireplaces, arbors, bars, and barbecue grilling stations will make you never want to leave the patio.

A firepit forms a central attraction in a patio designed with entertaining in mind. *Courtesy of Superlite Block, Inc.*

A whimsically curved riser on a double-stair to the patio is repeated at the next level beyond. A hot tub beckons weary muscles to hop in for a soothing soak. *Courtesy of Cambridge Pavers Inc.*

A built-in bench provides convenient seating for those who wish to gather around this patio's octagonal firepit. *Courtesy of Pavestone Company*

Successive spheres of brick draw attention to this backyard retreat. *Courtesy of Interlock Concrete Products, Inc.*

A cut-out in the center of this patio serves as a firepit for those cool, outdoor evenings. *Courtesy of Interlock Concrete Products, Inc.*

A circular firepit forms the central focal point for a radiating patio area.
Matching planters provide torch-like lighting and foliage. *Courtesy of
Barkman Concrete*

At night, the lights illuminate, adding romance and dimension. *Courtesy of Kerr Lighting*

Always entertaining friends on summer evenings, the owners of this patio installed lights in their retaining walls for practical and pretty reasons. *Courtesy of Kerr Lighting*

A pond set at the edge of the patio creates a special area for quiet contemplation and repose. *Courtesy of EP Henry*

Ragged edge pavers give this patio an aged feeling, gray and distinguished. The pond and chiminea are special features of this patio, where the owners spend many hours of relaxation. *Courtesy of Ideal Concrete Block Company, Inc.*
←

A bench constructed with driftwood has a rustic appeal that works in harmony with this patio's emphasis on the natural. A waterfall in the landscaped hill that borders the patio sings its water symphony night and day for a relaxing effect. *Courtesy of Genest Concrete*
→

A complex series of interlocking circles, half walls, and even a bridge make this patio feel like an adventure, luring explorers with the promise of surprises. *Courtesy of EP Henry*

Colorful flowers and a sprinkling fountain lure guests to the patio, where they'll stay for hours to enjoy the view and the company. *Courtesy of Bend Industries*

Red pavers demarcate boundaries on this patio and a broad descent to a parking area below. The living area near the home includes a wonderful, built-in cooking station. *Courtesy of Cambridge Pavers Inc.*

There's nothing quite like a good poolside cookout on the patio! *Courtesy of Paver Systems*

An extensive barbecue and food prep area serves as the modern day "summer kitchen," where the cook can crank out picnic feasts while escaping the heat. *Courtesy of EP Henry*

A built-in bar has the neighbors suffering patio envy. *Courtesy of Stonetown*

This patio countertop is the perfect amenity for any grilling guru. *Courtesy of EP Henry*

An extensive outdoor environment includes shelter, fire, water, and the luxury of a practice driving green and sand pit for the golfer. *Courtesy of EP Henry*

Circles of stone sneak into a bluish-gray rectangular patio, framing a cool and inviting pool. *Courtesy of R.I. Lampus*

An arbor provides décor to this patio entrance. Climbing vines will add greenery in the future. *Courtesy of Pavestone Company*

Rain needn't chase patio dwellers into the house; a screened-in pavilion beckons at the end of a short flight of stairs. *Courtesy of EP Henry*

Opposite page:
By placing the arbor at the patio's far edge, the owners achieved an even greater sense of space. An artful shelter provides shade and serves as a focal point for the outdoor living space, a gathering place in the center of the lawn. *Courtesy of Borgert Products*

Three seating options are offered the pavilion balcony, mezzanine level under the umbrella, or orchestra seats in lounge chairs. *Courtesy of EP Henry*

Stone arches and a central fireplace form a barrier between the civilized space of an expansive patio, and the wild beyond. *Courtesy of Borgert Products, Inc.*

contributors

Interlocking Concrete Pavement Institute (ICPI)
1444 I St., NW – Suite 700
Washington, DC 20005
202-712-9036/Fax: 202-408-0285
icpi@icpi.org
www.icpi.org

Abbotsford Concrete Products, Limited
3422 McCallum Road
Abbotsford, BC V2S 7W8 Canada
604-852-4967/Fax: 604-852-4819
abbcon@pavingstones.com
www.pavingstones.com

Angelus Block Co., Inc.
3435 S. Riverside Ave.
Rialto, CA 92316
909-328-9115/Fax: 909-321-0115
pavers@angelusblock.com
www.angelusblock.com

Barkman Concrete Ltd.
909 Gateway Road
Winnipeg MB R2K 3L1 Canada
204-667-3310/Fax: 204-663-4854
wpgsales@barkmanconcrete.com
www.barkmanconcrete.com

Basalite Concrete Products
11888 West Linne Rd.
Tracy, CA 95376
209-833-3670/Fax: 209-833-6039
bruce.camper@paccoast.com
www.basalitepavers.com

Belgard-Permacon, an Oldcastle Company
375 Northridge Road, Suite 250
Atlanta, GA 30350
770-804-3363/Fax: 770-804-3369
john.kemp@oldcastleapg.com
www.oldcastleapg.com

Bend Industries, an Oldcastle Company
2200 South Main Street
West Bend, WI 53905
262-338-5700/Fax: 262-306-8257
sales@bendind.com
www.bendindustries.com

Bolduc
1358 2nd Street Industrial Park
Ste. Marie, QC G6E 3B8 Canada
418-387-2634/Fax: 418-387-6438
info@bolduc.ca
www.bolduc.ca

Borgert Products
PO Box 39
St Joseph, MN 56374
320-363-4671/Fax: 320-363-8516
nolson@mail.borgertproducts.com
www.borgertproducts.com

Cambridge Pavers Inc.
P.O. Box 157
Lyndhurst, NJ 07071
201-933-5000/Fax: 201-933-5532
cambridge@cambridgepavers.com
www.cambridgepavers.com

EP Henry Corporation
PO Box 615
Woodbury, NJ 08096
800-444-3679/Fax: 856-845-0023
info@ephenry.com
www.ephenry.com

Flagstone Pavers
9070 Old Cobb Rd.
Brooksville, FL 34601
352-799-7933/Fax: 352-799-6844
gpb007@aol.com
www.flagstonepavers.com

Genest Concrete – Duracon Landscape Products
Wilson Street
PO Box 151
Sanford, ME 04073
207-324-3250/Fax: 207-490-5076
sales@genest-concrete.com
www.genest-concrete.com

Ideal Concrete Block Company, Inc.
PO Box 747
Westford, MA 01886
978-692-3076/Fax: 973-692-0817
www.idealconcreteblock.com

Interlock Concrete Products Inc.
3535 Bluff Drive
Jordan, MN 55352
952-492-3636
www.interlock-concrete.com
info@interlock-concrete.com

Interlock Paving Systems, Inc.
802 Pembroke Ave.
Hampton, VA 23669
757-723-0774/Fax: 757-723-8895
jhassell@interlockonline.com
www.interlockonline.com

Kerr Lighting
10 Soper Drive
PO Box 446
Smiths Falls, ON K7A 4T4 Canada
613-283-9571/Fax: 613-283-3828
info@kerrlighting.com
www.kerrlighting.com

Kirchner Block & Brick
12901 St. Charles Rock Rd.
Bridgeton, MO 63044
314-291-3200/Fax: 314-291-0265
sales@kirchnerblock.com
www.kirchnerblock.com

Mutual Materials Co.
605-119th NE
P.O. Box 2009
Bellevue, WA 98009
425-452-2300/Fax: 425-454-7732
ContactUs@mutualmaterials.com
www.mutualmaterials.com

Oaks Concrete Products
51744 Pontiac Trail
Wixom, MI 48393
248-684-5004/Fax: 248-684-2726
todd.rutledge@oakspaver.com
www.oakspavers.com

Oldcastle Architectural, Inc.
375 Northridge Rd. - Suite 350
Atlanta, GA 30350
770-804-3363/Fax: 770-804-3369
john.kemp@oldcastleapg.com
www.belgardhardscapes.co

Orco Block Company, Inc.
8042 Katella Ave.
Stanton, CA 90680
800-473-6726/Fax: 714-895-4021
mail@orco.com
www.orco.com

Paveloc Industries, Inc.
8302 South Route 23
Marengo, Illinois 60152
800-590-2772/Fax: 815-586-1210
www.paveloc.com

PaverModule
1590 North Andrews Ave. Extension
Pompano Beach, FL 33069
954-972-7400/Fax: 954-972-7433
info@pavermodule.com
www.pavermodule.com

Paver Systems LLC
7167 Interpace Road
West Palm Beach, FL 33407
561-844-5202
www.paversystems.com

Pavestone Company
4835 LBJ Freeway – Suite 700
Dallas, TX 75244
972-404-0400/Fax: 972-404-4379
www.pavestone.com

Peterson Brothers Construction
1560 W. Lambert Road
Brea, CA 92821
(714) 278-0488
info@pbc-online.com
www.pbc-online.com

R. I. Lampus Co.
816 RI Lampus Ave.
Springdale, PA 15144
412-362-3800/Fax: 724-274-2452
rilampus@lampus.com
www.lampus.com

RMC Concrete Products (UK) Limited
RMC House, Evreux Way
Rugby, Warks Cv21 2DT, United Kingdom
Webmanager.hbm@rmc.co.uk
www.rmc.co.uk

Site Technologies, Inc.
5090 Old Ellis Pointe – Suite A
Roswell, GA 30076
770-993-4344/Fax: 770-587-3042
beckman@sitetechnologies.com
www.sitetechnologies.com

Stonetown Construction Corp.
29 B Edison Ave
Oakland, NJ 07436
201-337-7773/Fax: 201-337-1248
robert@stonetownconstruction.com
www.stonetownconstruction.com

Techo-Bloc Inc.
5200 Albert–Millichamp
St-Hubert, QC J4X 1V5 Canada
450-556-2992/Fax: 450-656-1983
info@techo-bloc.com
www.techo-bloc.com

UNI-Group U.S.A.
4362 North Lake Blvd. Ste. 204
Palm Beach Gardens, FL 33410
800-872-1864/Fax: 561-627-6403
info@uni-groupusa.org
www.uni-groupusa.org

Unilock
301 E. Sullivan Road
Aurora, IL 60504
630-892-9191/Fax: 630-892-9215
unilock@unilock.com
www.unilock.com

Willamette Graystone Inc.
P.O. Box 68
2405 N.E. 244th Ave.
Troutdale, OR 97060
503-669-7612
www.willamettegraystone.com

PHOTO CREDITS:
*All PaverModule photographs by The Greg Wilson Group